OUIJA BOARD MAGICK - ARCHANGELS EDITION

Communicate And Harness The Power Of The Great Archangels

Copyright information

Copyright © 2015 by Baal Kadmon

All rights reserved. No part of this book may be reproduced by any mechanical, photographic, or electrical process, or in the form of a recording. Nor may it be stored in a storage/retrieval system nor transmitted or otherwise be copied for private or public use-other than "fair use" as quotations in articles or reviews—without the prior written consent of the Author.

The Information in this book is solely for educational purposes and not for the treatment, diagnosis or prescription of any diseases. This text is not meant to provide financial or health advice of any sort. The Author and the publisher are in no way liable for any use or misuse of the material. No Guarantee of results are being made in this text.

Kadmon, Baal

Ouija Board Magick - Archangels Edition- Communicate And Harness The Power Of The Great Archangels

–1st ed

Printed in the United States of America

Cover image : #80759621 | Author: dekanaryas- Fotolia.com

Book Cover Design: Baal Kadmon

At the best of our ability we have credited those who created the pictures based on the research we have conducted. If there are images in the book that have not been given due copyright notice please

contact us at Resheph@baalkadmon.com and we will remedy the situation by giving proper copyright credit or we will remove the image/s at your request.

Dedication

This book is dedicated to the great and holy Archangels

Introduction

From time immemorial, people have been wanting to communicate with the great unknown. We all know instinctively that there is a reality beyond what we can see. We feel it, we sense it and just know that we are not alone in this world. I am not talking about little green men (although they too exist) but I am talking in a supernatural world that is beyond our senses, yet in a real way very accessible by the senses themselves. If you read any spiritual tradition you will find countless worlds of spiritual beings, from archangels , demons, fairies, elementals and so on. And ever since, we have sought their guidance, their protection or their repulsion. More often than not, we are looking to them for guidance. We pray, we fast, we sing, we dance and we use such devices as the Ouija board in order to communicate with them.

In this series " Ouija Board Magick" we will discuss the various ways of communicating with the spiritual world. Each volume will contain one class of spiritual beings. We will learn what they are and brief history of both the spiritual entities and the Ouija board, as well as ways to harness their powers for our magickal purposes.

But I must warn you, this is certainly not for the faint of heart. Using a Ouija board is , even for people such as myself who practice magick on a daily basis a slight bit " spooky". When using the Ouija you are opening a portal to the unknown.

In this book, we will discuss how to communicate and work magickally with the Archangels of the western tradition; Mainly Angels Michael, Gabriel, Uriel , Raphael and one other Angel Metatron.

Ouija Boards And Its Antecedence

It might seem odd that I would be writing a book about Ouija boards. After all, most people consider it a children's game. Some of the top toy manufactures produced their own versions of the Ouija board . It is considered a nice spooky game that most age groups can enjoy during Halloween night. The thing is, it is in fact a much more serious thing than just a harmless game. Despite what many say, the Ouija board can be a very powerful tool for spiritual communications. Now I would also like to mention that some of the perceived dangers of Ouija board usage is a bit hyped. Rest Assured, You will not get possessed by demons and noxious devils such Baalzebub or Asmodeus, and you most certainly wont have green vomit coming out of you nor will you be committing gross acts of debauchery and sacrilege because of it. Sorry, I know some may find demonic possession cool but in this book I will certainly not teach or condone that...Well, not in this particular book anyway :).

Before we proceed, let me give you a brief history of Ouija boards. I think it is always important to know some background before you perform any kind of spiritual work, no matter what it entails.

As I mentioned above, the Ouija board was first introduced as a simple game. It was put into production by a businessman, Elijah Bonds in 1890 and released in 1894. He was certainly capitalizing on a spiritualism craze that swept the nation and much of Europe. People such as the Great Madam Blavatsky and her decimation of all things occult, and who highly condoned the art of mediumship or the capability to communicate directly with spiritual forces. Elijah certainly knew of the interest in spiritual communication that HP Blavatsky promoted so well. I suppose it is no coincidence she died a year AFTER the Ouija Board was introduced.

The concept of the Ouija board is fairly simple, you ask a question of the spiritual entities and they guide your hands to various parts of the board that have either " Yes Or No" answers, the spirit can also answer using alpha numeric as well since the entire alphabets and the numbers 1-9 and 0 are on the board as well. Its popularity grew and was a common tool for divining during the first world war.

In essence, what the Ouija board is, is a method of automatic writing. A phenomenon that entails a spiritual entity guiding ones hands to form sentences and writing with specific messages. It's a very popular mode of spiritual communication and is used extensively to this day. Many Channeled works are either directly using automatic writing or have been influenced by it.

One might think that Ouija board is a decidedly western invention and yes, the modern rendition is surely western, but the use of Ouija board-like methods have been used for quite some time.

Let us go back to Liu Song Dynasty China around 420-479 AD, it was at this point where we find one of the very first mentioning of "Spirit writing" also known to modern scholars as "Fuji-Planchette Writing". Its from that point, the spirit writing became incredibly popular. It peaked during the Ming Dynasty around 1522-1566 and was then banned during the Qing Dynasty, 1644-1912. Although it was banned, it is still used in certain temples in the east; especially amongst Taoist practitioners. Fuji-Planchette Writing used a suspended tray to guide a stick which would write Chinese charters in the ashes of incense or sand on its own.

There are of course other means of divining the spiritual entities, but automatic writing is a very direct way. In this book, we will be using Automatic writing via the Ouija board using the Archangels. In many ways the rituals in this book are more for reception of information from the archangels. In many ways I am combining basic ritual magick with Ouija board usage. I am sure you will find it very useful. Before we go into the rituals, let us discuss a bit more.

Angelic Beings

In every single spiritual tradition there are spiritual entities called Angels. Of course they may not all use the term "Angel" itself, but they are for all intents and purposes angels as we know them in the western tradition.

The word angel is derived from the Green "Angelos" which means messenger. In Hebrew the word for angel is Malach which also has the same meaning.

Generally speaking, Angels are spiritual beings without a physical form. Although the bible and other spiritual texts describe them with wings and other limbs. They are, in essence, pure divine energy. The reason they are described with a body is so we can experience their energy with our senses. Since we are sensory driven, the angels will cloth themselves in ways that would allow us to interact and identify them.

As I stated earlier, Angels are messengers and helpers of God. Every angel has its purpose. For example, the archangel Raphael is Gods servant of healing. The major angels are constantly relaying Gods divine energy through them for us and the universe in general. Some angels do this work for all eternity while some angels are created for one purpose and mission and when that mission is complete, they no longer exists.

In Jewish tradition it is said that whenever a person does a good deed, they "create" an angelic advocate. This also applies if a person does an evil deed; they create an angelic accuser. These angel advocates are created from the mental and emotional energy you expend when you commit the act.

The angels we will be calling in this text are known as archangels. Archangels are generally considered the highest of all the angelic orders. This is the common idea that runs through all the western religions, mainly, Judaism, Christianity and Islam; the Abrahamic traditions as it were. Angels such as Gabriel, Raphael, Michael and Uriel are most common. I will include the Angel Metatron as well. (We will discuss those above in a bit). In Islam, the archangels are also Gabriel and Michael but differ with the others. The other two in Islam are Azrael and Israfil. Some traditions mention that there are 4 archangels and some 7. For our purposes, we will discuss 5; 1 I have added since I feel he is very important. Although we will be discussing mostly the Archangels as they are known within the Western traditions, the idea of archangels can also be found in other religions.

One religion that has a discernible archangelic structure is Zoroastrianism. In many ways, some would say that the concept of archangel proceeded from Zoroastrianism and later found itself in the western traditions. I tend to think this idea has substantial merit, it is for this reason I will touch upon the Zoroastrian notion for just a bit.

In Zoroastrianism, these archangels are called "Amesha Spentas" . 7 in total.

1. Spenta Mainyu - 'Bountiful Spirit'
2. Asha Vahishta - 'Highest Truth'

3. Vohu Mano - 'Righteous Mind'
4. Khshathra Vairya - 'Desirable Dominion'
5. Spenta Armaiti - 'Holy Devotion'
6. Haurvatat - 'Perfection or Health'
7. Ameretat - 'Immortality'

When the creator God Ahura Mazda created the universe, he created these angels to look over the entire of earthly creation aka the 16 lands as it is called. . The Amesha Spentas were charged with protecting these lands and through their power, also exert influence on the residence there in. As in the western tradition, they are to help guide humanity towards the light. If you want a good book on the Zoroastrianism, I highly recommend "Zoroastrians: Their Religious Beliefs and Practices by Mary Boyce" it a nice introduction, can be slightly academic at times, but worth the read.

In the next chapter, I will introduce you to the 5 archangels we will be using.

The Mighty Archangels

I shall now introduce you to the 5 archangels we will be working with. I will give a brief description of each and then we will proceed to the rituals. These angels are very powerful and I am confident they will communicate with you directly, even within the first ritual.

Archangel Michael

Michael is by far the most well-known Archangel. In the biblical tradition he is considered to be the great warrior angel and "the great prince". As a warrior angel he is in charge of making sure that Gods divine will is fulfilled. It is not clear exactly what name Michael means. Some say it means "Who Is Like God", but that is often followed by a Question mark. It is simply not clear. Throughout the bible, specifically the Old Testament he is the guardian angel of the Jewish people. He is, of course the guardian of all.

In Christian tradition, he is the angel that cast Lucifer (later known as Satan) out from heaven. In the tradition, Lucifer would defy God and evil and therefore Michael, which I guess you could say is Lucifer's opposite banished him.

Magickally speaking: He is used for several areas of life. First and foremost protection from evil people and any malevolence be it spiritual or human. He is an establisher of peace and harmony in all areas of life. For our purposes we will use him for protection again evil of all sorts.

His Day of Week: Sunday

His Candle color: Blue, Gold and Black.

Archangel Gabriel

The Name Gabriel means the strength of God or "Gods Hero". It's interesting to note that although his name indicates strength, it is the not the kind of strength that Michael has. One would think that Michael should be Gods hero. But the true strength of God is his message. Thus Gabriel is truly "the strength of God". Why? He is the angel used to communicate divine messages. He is Gods messenger. He is found within all western traditions, Judaism, Christy and Islam and in all traditions he is the one that conveys special divine messages. He communicated with Mary telling her she would give birth to Jesus. He communicated the Quran to the prophet Muhammad.

Magickally speaking: He is used for several areas of life. However for our purposes in this book we will contact him for divine wisdom. You can also call upon him for anything you need clarity on.

His Day of Week: Monday

His Candle color: White, Silver.

Archangel Uriel

The name Uriel means " God is My Light". Uriel, I feel does not get as much credit for what he represents. He is the angel that helps one achieve pure consciousness. He can help shift our natural tendency of pessimism into optimism. He can take any perceived disappointments in our lives and turn it around. I guess you could say he is the angel of impossible causes. He is most often mentioned in rabbinic and Christian traditions. He is also found very often in apocryphal literature as well. Such as the book of Enoch, book of Esdras, Apocalypse of Peter etc. The Anglican Liturgical calendar day that celebrates the archangels has a beautiful prayer to him.

> *"Oh holy Saint Uriel, intercede for us that our hearts may burn with the fire of the Sacred Heart of Jesus.*
>
> *Assist us in co-operating with the graces of our*
> *confirmation that the gifts of the*
> *Holy Spirit may bear much fruit in our souls.*
> *Obtain for us the grace to use the sword of truth to pare*
> *away all that is not in conformity to the most adorable*
> *Will of God in our lives, that we may fully participate in the*
> *army of the Church*
> *Amen*

Saint Uriel Church website patron Saint web page. Retrieved September 15, 2008.

Above all else, he is the angel of forgiveness, not only for what we have done to others, but what we do to ourselves. In this book we will tap into this angel to give us peace of mind and self-forgiveness. If you are to be a magician of any worth, you must be clear of heart.

His Day of Week: Saturday

His Candle color: Blue

Archangel Raphael

Right up there with the angels Michael and Gabriel, Angel Raphael is one of the most popular archangels. In Hebrew, Raphael means, the "healer of God". He has been historically used to bring mental and physical healing. Raphael himself is not mentioned directly in the bible but is often considered to have played a major role in it. He was the one who healed Jacob after wrestling with the angel of God. He was the one who gave calm and healing to Sarah in regards to her conception. Some even say that he bestowed upon Solomon the spirit-binding and magickal ring which is often referenced in ceremonial magick texts. Texts that I personally do not feel are valid, but this book is not about that.

For our purposes, we will use this angel for healing physical ailments. You can use him to heal yourself or others.

His Day of Week: Wednesday

His Candle color: Blue, white, Red

Archangel Metatron

Metatron is not in the official archangel lists, but he is one in the kabalistic traditions. In many ways, he is an angel for all things. You can use him for whatever it is you like. Metatron, like Uriel can often be found in the book of Enoch and other apocryphal books. There is not much known of him, but many think that he was the ancient Enoch from the book of genesis, the first man to have been taken up by God without physically dying and once he reached the heavens he turned into the angel Metatron.

Metatron in Greek means "Behind The Throne", meaning he is an angel that works behind the scenes. He is the main angel that drives the divine energy. I guess in many ways you could say he is the right hand of God. Since he is not only the angel of knowledge but the possessor of divine energy, he can be used for whatever purpose you require. For our purpose, we will use Metatron the archangel for brining in abundance into our lives, but only for our highest good.

His Day of Week: Any Day of the Week

His Candle color: All colors, but Gold and Silver are what we will use.

Ways To Enhance Ouija Board Magick

Here are a few things I think are needed to work Ouija Board Magick. These are all option save, of course the Ouija board itself. Here is a list of items that can help your Magick.

1. Ouija Board, I suspect that is the most obvious. The **"Classic Ouija Board"** will do. You can even make your own if you like. I use the standard classic. I do intend to create my own at some point. If you are interested please write to resheph@baalkadmon.com if you would be interested in one I will create.

2. Novena cards or statues of the angels. I just happen to have these 5 statutes:

A. Metatron Bronze Satute

B. Angel Michael Statue

C. Angel Gabriel

D. Angel Raphael

E. Angel Uriel

These Statutes are a little costly. However, You can use any ones you like , even just pictures of the angels. It really doesn't matter. I just like to use them because it helps me focus my attention and these are very nice depictions.

3. **Frankincense and Myrrh:** This Incense is a wonderful sacred fragrance and was once more precious than gold. It was so valuable that people would rather it than gold itself. I find the fragrance holy and fitting for this work.

4. **Candles: (Please note you can buy any kind of candle you like, they don't have to be chimes or votive. I just happen to like the ones I provided here)**

Red Chime Candles: This color is quite powerful.

Gold Candles: This candle will be used for the ritual on financial assistance. Many occultists will tell you to use green, but this has been a long-held misconception. The only reason why people have said to use green is because it's the color of money. The thing is, it's only the color of money in the USA and maybe a few notes here and there of other nations. They don't call the dollar "greenback" for nothing. Green is not a color that is truly indicative money. Gold is though, Gold is UNIVERSALLY known to be a signifier of wealth both in ancient times and present. If you have been using Green for your money rituals, now you know to use gold instead. It is much more effective.

White Candles: White is for purity and will be used for our ritual for inner peace.

Silver candles: This is the of wisdom and will be used for ritual on divine wisdom that only certain angels can bestow. As well as for magickal powers.

<u>Blue Candles</u>: This will be used for health

<u>Black Candles</u>: These candles will be used to conquer your enemies and repel evil spiritual entities.

5. Any bible with a book of Psalms will do.

6. A Notebook to record any messages you might receive. I use this one only because I love the aesthetic, <u>Vintage Dark Green PU Leather Cover Loose</u> any notebook or pad will do.

7. (Optional) <u>A Sony Digital Flash Recorder</u> (or other digital recorder). I use this at times when I do not want to write. Sometimes writing can be distracting, especially if the message is long. You may want to record yourself as angelic messages come through you. I just happen to like the <u>Sony Digital Flash recorder</u>. ..Any brand will do.

As you can see, these few items are not complicated, as I mentioned, you can use all of these or none, the only thing you really do need is the Ouija board of course.

Ouija Board Magick - The Rituals

You will find that the magick contained herein is quite straight forward and easy. Although the below this might not seem like Magick, it actually is. When you call the angels in this way THEY will provide you what you need to do to achieve your intention. Most people feel the performance of Magick means things will just pop out of thin air, this is not always true, GUIDANCE is also a result of Magick. This is what we are looking for here.

One might ask, why do we even need the Ouija board? The reason is the angels will often give you a message as it relates to the issues at hand as I stated above. Of course, you can use these angels for whatever you want, but to make this book easier to read, we will focus on the just a few topics.

1. Protection

2. Wisdom And Intuition

3. Peace of Mind

4. Physical Healing

5. Prosperity.

Basic Instructions: I will repeat them with every ritual, this way you have all the information you need at all times.

1. If you have an altar large enough to place all the items that is great,

but in reality, any table will do.

Please setup the table or Altar as such

Incense

Candles   Angel Statue Or Image   Candle

Ouija Board

If it is easier for you to place the Ouija Board on your lap that is fine as well. I understand that sometimes it may not be comfortable actually sitting at an altar , especially if the altar is too high or low. If you need to sit on your bed or another place that is fine as well. But you MUST at least be facing your altar when you do this. **You may light the candles and incense at any time before you start the ritual.**

2. Take out the book of Psalms and turn to the psalms that corresponds to the angel.

3. If you have a notebook, please place it by your side in the event you get a message that needs to be written down. You can also keep a digital recorder I mentioned above during the ritual so you don't need to write . Whatever works for you.

4. Sit quietly and take in the incense and the candle light, just be in the moment.

5. Read the Psalms. I will provide the text for the psalms here as well.

6. Invoke the Angel and allow the angel to arrive. You WILL feel the presence.

7. State the intention of your ritual

8. Place your hands on the Ouija board

9. Take Heed of what the angel tells you through the Ouija Board. The Angel will give you guidance on the intention you have stated.

10. Thank the angel and bid it leave in peace.

You may sit with the Ouija board past this point to see if you get other insights. That's pretty much it, You will notice that contact will be fairly easy.

Angel Michael - Protection.

ON A SUNDAY

LET US BEGIN

Incense

Candles   Angel Statue Or Image   Candle

Ouija Board

1. Light the Blue and Black candles and the incense

2. Open to Psalms 91

3. Keep notebook or recorder at hand

4. sit with the candles, incense and angelic image, just take it in. Feel The peace.

5. Read Psalms 91 NIV Bible verses below.

"¹ Whoever dwells in the shelter of the Most High
    will rest in the shadow of the Almighty
² I will say of the LORD, "He is my refuge and my fortress,
    my God, in whom I trust."

³ Surely he will save you
    from the fowler's snare
    and from the deadly pestilence.
⁴ He will cover you with his feathers,
    and under his wings you will find refuge;
    his faithfulness will be your shield and rampart.
⁵ You will not fear the terror of night,
    nor the arrow that flies by day,
⁶ nor the pestilence that stalks in the darkness,
    nor the plague that destroys at midday.
⁷ A thousand may fall at your side,
    ten thousand at your right hand,
    but it will not come near you.
⁸ You will only observe with your eyes
    and see the punishment of the wicked.

⁹ If you say, "The LORD is my refuge,"
    and you make the Most High your dwelling,

¹⁰ no harm will overtake you,

    no disaster will come near your tent.

¹¹ For he will command his angels concerning you

    to guard you in all your ways;

¹² they will lift you up in their hands,

    so that you will not strike your foot against a stone.

¹³ You will tread on the lion and the cobra;

    you will trample the great lion and the serpent.

¹⁴ "Because he[b] loves me," says the Lord, "I will rescue him;

    I will protect him, for he acknowledges my name.

¹⁵ He will call on me, and I will answer him;

    I will be with him in trouble,

    I will deliver him and honor him.

¹⁶ With long life I will satisfy him

    and show him my salvation."

6. Invoke the Angel " **Oh Mighty Archangel Michael come to me and provide me the protection I so desire. oh blessed angel of the Lord**"

7. State the intention of your ritual

8. Place your hands on the Ouija board

9. Take Heed of what the angel tells you through the Ouija Board. The Angel will give you guidance on the intention you have stated. He may

also give you advice as to whom to avoid in your life and those who may have malice against you.

10. Thank the angel and bid it leave in peace.

You may sit with the Ouija board past this point to see if you get other insights. That's pretty much it, You will notice that contact will be fairly easy.

Angel Gabriel - Wisdom and Intuition.

ON A MONDAY

LET US BEGIN

Incense

Candles   Angel Statue Or Image   Candle

Ouija Board

1. Light the White and Silver candles and the incense

2. Open to Psalms 39

3. Keep notebook or recorder at hand

4. sit with the candles, incense and angelic image, just take it in. Feel The peace.

5. Read Psalms 39 NIV Bible verses below.

For the director of music. For Jeduthun. A psalm of David.

¹ I said, "I will watch my ways
   and keep my tongue from sin;
I will put a muzzle on my mouth
   while in the presence of the wicked."
² So I remained utterly silent,
   not even saying anything good.
But my anguish increased;
³   my heart grew hot within me.
While I meditated, the fire burned;
   then I spoke with my tongue:

⁴ "Show me, LORD, my life's end
   and the number of my days;
   let me know how fleeting my life is.
⁵ You have made my days a mere handbreadth;
   the span of my years is as nothing before you.
Everyone is but a breath,
   even those who seem secure.[b]

⁶ "Surely everyone goes around like a mere phantom;
   in vain they rush about, heaping up wealth
   without knowing whose it will finally be.

⁷ "But now, Lord, what do I look for?
   My hope is in you.
⁸ Save me from all my transgressions;
   do not make me the scorn of fools.
⁹ I was silent; I would not open my mouth,
   for you are the one who has done this.
¹⁰ Remove your scourge from me;
   I am overcome by the blow of your hand.
¹¹ When you rebuke and discipline anyone for their sin,
   you consume their wealth like a moth—
   surely everyone is but a breath.

¹² "Hear my prayer, LORD,
   listen to my cry for help;
   do not be deaf to my weeping.
I dwell with you as a foreigner,
   a stranger, as all my ancestors were.
¹³ Look away from me, that I may enjoy life again
   before I depart and am no more."

6. Invoke the Angel " **Oh Mighty Archangel Gabriel come to me and provide me the wisdom I so desire. oh blessed angel of the Lord"**

7. State the intention of your ritual

8. Place your hands on the Ouija board

9. Take Heed of what the angel tells you through the Ouija Board. The Angel will give you guidance and hidden wisdom. **This is a very powerful ritual.**

10. Thank the angel and bid it leave in peace.

You may sit with the Ouija board past this point to see if you get other insights.

Angel Uriel - Peace Of Mind

ON A SATURDAY

LET US BEGIN

Incense

Candles   Angel Statue Or Image   Candle

Ouija Board

1. Light the Blue candles and the incense

2. Open to Psalms 23

3. Keep notebook or recorder at hand

4. sit with the candles, incense and angelic image, just take it in. Feel The peace.

5. Read Psalms 23 NIV Bible verses below.

A psalm of David.

[1] The Lord is my shepherd, I lack nothing.
[2]   He makes me lie down in green pastures,
he leads me beside quiet waters,
[3]   he refreshes my soul.
He guides me along the right paths
   for his name's sake.
[4] Even though I walk
   through the darkest valley,[a]
I will fear no evil,
   for you are with me;
your rod and your staff,
   they comfort me.

[5] You prepare a table before me
   in the presence of my enemies.
You anoint my head with oil;
   my cup overflows.
[6] Surely your goodness and love will follow me
   all the days of my life,
and I will dwell in the house of the Lord
   forever.

6. Invoke the Angel " **Oh Mighty Archangel Uriel come to me , please pray to God on my behalf that I may acquire peace of mind over the issue of _____ (Fill in the Blank)**

7. State the intention of your ritual

8. Place your hands on the Ouija board

9. Take Heed of what the angel tells you through the Ouija Board. The Angel will give you the guidance you need to attain peace of mind. He may give you the exact steps you need to make your life better and more peaceful and to banish your fears.

10. Thank the angel and bid it leave in peace.

You may sit with the Ouija board past this point to see if you get other insights.

Angel Raphael - Physical Healing

ON A WEDNESDAY

LET US BEGIN

Incense

Candles Angel Statue Or Image Candle

Ouija Board

1. Light the White and Red candles and the incense

2. Open to Psalms 30

3. Keep notebook or recorder at hand

4. sit with the candles, incense and angelic image, just take it in. Feel The peace.

5. Read Psalms 30 NIV Bible verses below.

¹ I will exalt you, Lord,
   for you lifted me out of the depths
   and did not let my enemies gloat over me.
² Lord my God, I called to you for help,
   and you healed me.
³ You, Lord, brought me up from the realm of the dead;
   you spared me from going down to the pit.

⁴ Sing the praises of the Lord, you his faithful people;
   praise his holy name.
⁵ For his anger lasts only a moment,
   but his favor lasts a lifetime;
weeping may stay for the night,
   but rejoicing comes in the morning.

⁶ When I felt secure, I said,
   "I will never be shaken."
⁷ Lord, when you favored me,
   you made my royal mountain[c] stand firm;
but when you hid your face,
   I was dismayed.

[8] To you, LORD, I called;

   to the Lord I cried for mercy:

[9] "What is gained if I am silenced,

   if I go down to the pit?

Will the dust praise you?

   Will it proclaim your faithfulness?

[10] Hear, LORD, and be merciful to me;

   LORD, be my help."

[11] You turned my wailing into dancing;

   you removed my sackcloth and clothed me with joy,

[12] that my heart may sing your praises and not be silent.

   LORD my God, I will praise you forever.

6. Invoke the Angel " **Oh Mighty Archangel Raphael come to me , please help heal the physical ailment _____ (Fill in the Blank) that I have. Please Angel Raphael. I trust in you.**

7. State the intention of your ritual

8. Place your hands on the Ouija board

9. Take Heed of what the angel tells you through the Ouija Board. The Angel will give you the guidance you need to attain health, he might tell you what you need to hear. I have had direct messages regarding an issue I had and it was so true. This is a very powerful ritual. Raphael is

such a gentle force.

10. Thank the angel and bid it leave in peace.

You may sit with the Ouija board past this point to see if you get other insights.

Angel Metatron - Material Abundance

ON ANY DAY YOU LIKE

LET US BEGIN

Incense

Candles   Angel Statue Or Image   Candle

Ouija Board

1. Light the Gold and Silver candles and the incense

2. Open to Psalms 85

3. Keep notebook or recorder at hand

4. sit with the candles, incense and angelic image, just take it in. Feel The peace.

5. Read Psalms 85 NIV Bible verses below.

For the director of music. Of the Sons of Korah. A psalm.

¹ You, Lord, showed favor to your land;
   you restored the fortunes of Jacob.
² You forgave the iniquity of your people
   and covered all their sins.
³ You set aside all your wrath
   and turned from your fierce anger.

⁴ Restore us again, God our Savior,
   and put away your displeasure toward us.
⁵ Will you be angry with us forever?
   Will you prolong your anger through all generations?
⁶ Will you not revive us again,
   that your people may rejoice in you?
⁷ Show us your unfailing love, Lord,
   and grant us your salvation.

⁸ I will listen to what God the Lord says;
   he promises peace to his people, his faithful servants—
   but let them not turn to folly.
⁹ Surely his salvation is near those who fear him,
   that his glory may dwell in our land.

¹⁰ Love and faithfulness meet together;

    righteousness and peace kiss each other.

¹¹ Faithfulness springs forth from the earth,

    and righteousness looks down from heaven.

¹² The LORD will indeed give what is good,

    and our land will yield its harvest.

¹³ Righteousness goes before him

    and prepares the way for his steps.

6. Invoke the Angel " **Oh Mighty Archangel Metatron come to me , I know that the manifestation of Material abundance is easy for you. Please bless me with material abundance for my good and the good of all Amen.**

7. State the intention of your ritual

8. Place your hands on the Ouija board

9. Take Heed of what the angel tells you through the Ouija Board. He might give you an idea for a business for guidance on how to enhance you material wealth. Please do not fear, he will help you manifest it for the good of all.

10. Thank the angel and bid it leave in peace.

You may sit with the Ouija board past this point to see if you get other insights.

Conclusion

This concludes Volume 1 of the Ouija Board Magick - using the Archangels. As you have seen, it is quite simple. There is no pomp and circumstance, no expensive ritual garments and paraphernalia, no odd and impossible herbs to obtain, no directions to turn to, no contrived and pompous terminology and phrases. Just pure, honest Magick using the Ouija Board and the Archangels. I am filled with utmost confidence that once you have preformed one of these rituals, you will enter a magickal partnership with the blessed angels. I am also convinced that after you use the Ouija board in this manner, you will be using it again and again .

Please note that it is okay for your to perform these rituals. It is not a sin and never will be. It is a divine and sacred art and will be forevermore.

Other Books By The Author

The Mantra Magick Series:

VASHIKARAN MAGICK - LEARN THE DARK MANTRAS OF SUBJUGATION

Kali Mantra Magick: Summoning The Dark Powers of Kali Ma

Seed Mantra Magick: Master The Primordial Sounds of The universe

Chakra Mantra Magick: Tap Into The Magick Of Your Chakras

The Scared Names Series:

THE 72 NAMES OF GOD - THE 72 KEYS OF TRANSFORMATION

THE 72 ANGELS OF THE NAME - CALLING ON THE 72 ANGELS OF GOD

THE 99 NAMES OF ALLAH - ACQUIRING THE 99 DIVINE QUALITIES OF GOD

THE HIDDEN NAMES OF GENESIS - TAP INTO THE HIDDEN POWER OF MANIFESTATION

Magick Of the Saints Series

Mary Magick: Calling Forth The Divine Mother For Help

The Magick of Saint Expedite: Tap Into the Truly Miraculous Power of Saint Expedite

DISCLAIMER

Disclaimer: By law, I need to add this statement.

This volume of " Ouija Board Magick" is for educational purposes only and does not claim to prevent or cure any disease. The advice and methods in this book should not be construed as financial ,medical or psychological treatment. Please seek advice from a professional if you have serious financial, medical or psychological issues.

By purchasing , reading and or listening to this book, you understand that results are not guaranteed. In light of this, you understand that in the event that this book or audio does not work or causes harm in any area of your life, you agree that you do not hold Baal Kadmon, Amazon, its employees or affiliates liable for any damages you may experience or incur.

The Text and or Audio in this series are copyrighted 2015

Printed in Great Britain
by Amazon